Maria-D. Kokerud/
Cothigham

25 -03.

31/98

# A BOND HONOURED

## Other Plays by John Osborne

\*

LUTHER

INADMISSIBLE EVIDENCE

A PATRIOT FOR ME

LOOK BACK IN ANGER

THE ENTERTAINER

PLAYS FOR ENGLAND:
*The Blood of the Bambergs* and *Under Plain Cover*
THE WORLD OF PAUL SLICKEY

A SUBJECT OF SCANDAL AND CONCERN:
A play for television
EPITAPH FOR GEORGE DILLON
(with Anthony Creighton)
TOM JONES: A FILMSCRIPT

# A BOND HONOURED

## A Play

by
## JOHN OSBORNE
*(from Lope De Vega)*

## FABER AND FABER
24 Russell Square
London

*First published in mcmlxvi*
*by Faber and Faber Limited*
*24 Russell Square London WC1*
*Printed in Great Britain by*
*Latimer Trend & Co Ltd Plymouth*
*All rights reserved*

© 1966 by John Osborne

The first performance of A BOND
HONOURED was given at The National
Theatre, Waterloo Road, London, on
June 6th 1966 by the National Theatre
Company. It was directed by John Dexter
and the decor was by Michael Annals.
The musical advisor was Marc Wilkinson.
The cast was as follows:

| | |
|---|---|
| Dionisio | MICHAEL BYRNE |
| Berlebeyo | GRAHAM CROWDEN |
| Gerardo | PAUL CURRAN |
| Lidora | JANINA FAYE |
| Tizon | GERALD JAMES |
| Marcela | MAGGIE SMITH |
| Leonido | ROBERT STEPHENS |

## AUTHOR'S NOTE

In 1963, Kenneth Tynan, Literary Manager of the National Theatre, asked me if I would adapt *La Fianza Satisfecha* by Lope de Vega. It was in three acts, had an absurd plot, some ridiculous characters and some very heavy humour. What did interest me was the Christian framework of the play and the potentially fascinating dialectic with the principal character. So I concentrated on his development (in the original he rapes his sister in the opening moments of the play without any preparatory explanation of his character or circumstances) and discarded most of the rest, reducing the play to one long act.

*A Bond Honoured* is the result.

J. O.

# CHARACTERS

## CAST

LEONIDO
TIZON            *His Servant*
DIONISIO         *His brother-in-law. Husband*
                 *of Marcela*
GERARDO          *His father*
BERLEBEYO        *Moorish King*
MARCELA          *Sister of Leonido*
ZULEMA           *A Moor*
ZARRABULLI       *A Moor*
LIDORA           *A Moorish Lady*
MAID

## ACT ONE

## ACT TWO

# ACT ONE

## SCENE 1

*All the actors in the play sit immobile in a circle through-out most of the action. When those who are all in the same scene rise to take part in it, they all do so together. Long cloaks should be worn. The acting style is hard to discover or describe. I will just say: it must be extremely violent, pent-up, toppling on and over the edge of animal howlings and primitive rage. At the same time, it should have an easy, modern naturalness, even in the most extravagant or absurd moments. It requires actors like athletes who behave like conversationalists. It is not impossible or as difficult as it sounds. We English are more violent than we allow ourselves to know. That is why we have the greatest body of dramatic literature in the world.*

*Sicily.* GERARDO's *garden by the sea.* TIZON, *a servant, lies asleep.*

VOICE OFF : Tizon! Tizon!
> *Enter* LEONIDO.
LEONIDO : Tizon! Tizon—why, of course, of course asleep. All easy aren't you, snoozing? Like a basket of old laundry, mucky and no use to anyone. Wake up! Up!
TIZON : Master! I fell asleep.
LEONIDO : Tizon, when you sleep, you should do it under cover, in a hole or some cellar. Your sleeping's like your eating and most other things about you. It's better not looked on. When you just swallow a glass of wine the

15

effect's like the dead stink of a bat dropped into a well. As for your other functions, I daren't think of them. But to find you *asleep*, all mess and remains like some decomposing beast, by the roadside, is so hateful to anyone awake to life itself, itself—you're lucky I didn't kill you.

TIZON: Forgive me.

LEONIDO: I can't forgive what I can't remake. Asleep! Why! You watch me when it suits your book.

TIZON: It was late, my lord.

LEONIDO: It's not late by my clock, and that is the one *you* live by. My heartbeat's the one you pay heed to. Your own's not worth keeping up for. You keep up for mine. It's more than you deserve, but it's what you've got and then you go and leave me when I'm alone and awake and waiting. Why? Eh?

TIZON: I was tired.

LEONIDO: Tired. Why? Tizon?—Are you tired?

TIZON: I don't know.

LEONIDO: No, you don't. Why should you be tired, you onlooker? You do nothing. And you're not furniture—nor decoration. There's no sweat in watching. I—I live for you, Tizon. You have nothing to do, nothing to expend. Busy little lard bundles should keep awake during the intervals and dull bits. Hear me! Keep awake and stay with me. And give me that wine. Is Dionisio gone yet?

TIZON: He's still with your father.

LEONIDO: How do you know, you don't even know you stink, you rumbling, drowsy equivocator?

TIZON: I——

16

LEONIDO: You don't. You're flailing aren't you?

TIZON: I am sure——

LEONIDO: No. Not *am* sure.

TIZON: I was watching——

LEONIDO: Am *not* sure.

TIZON: Master——

LEONIDO: You're dishonest, treacherous and you even botch treachery worse than most other men. Not *am* sure, Tizon.

TIZON: Yes.

LEONIDO: What?

TIZON: Yes, master.

LEONIDO: Yes, to what? What? Yes? You don't know. You back it as easily as "no" if you think it'll come up. Don't know. Not watching—for once. The thing one should at least demand from a fool is stamina. Get up! (*Kicks him.*) Tell me, no, not why, how, how can you sleep so much? Hey? When I've not slept for three nights?

TIZON: I don't know.

LEONIDO: Three nights since I slept and then only for a few minutes before I was tipped out by my sister.

TIZON: Sh!

LEONIDO: Sh what! Tipped out before her closing up time at dawn. What is it, why are you squinting and winking like some bit of bridal bait in the dark?

TIZON: My lord!

LEONIDO: You're like my sister. Ah, there's her light. Gone to bed already to get away from the tedium of her betrothed. Bridal bait. Marcela! Marcela! Gone to bed? Bridal bait!

B                                  17

TIZON: My lord, I beg you!

LEONIDO: Her maid's drawn her curtain. She sees herself as a bride guard too. What are you begging?

TIZON: Be circumspect.

LEONIDO: About?

TIZON: What may or may not in the past, that is, have occurred between you and your sister. Now that she's to be a bride——

LEONIDO: Not may or may not have. Has. Did. Is. Not was, might, may. *Is.* Well?

TIZON: It's unkind to pollute Dionisio's opinion of his bride. As well as your father's affection for his daughter——

LEONIDO: As for Dionisio's minced opinions about my sister or any other object—they could only interest my father by their enormity of dullness.

TIZON: Then think of yourself, Leonido.

LEONIDO: Leonido, is it?

TIZON: Your reputation. I'm sorry.

LEONIDO: Don't be. Leonido was good for a moment. You almost creaked into life there, old fat bones, blown up bones, yes they are, why your bones have turned, so they have, they've simmered into gristle and jelly there, from all that sleep. From sleep that babyish dreaming in the belly that fishy swimming in mother's old moorings.

TIZON: Stop!

LEONIDO: Stop! Does your mother know you're back in there again?

TIZON: What is it? Do you want no man's good opinion.

LEONIDO: Not yours!

18

TIZON: No! Not mine.

LEONIDO: Good! First Leonido, now some more exertion. Is it only what the world thinks that stops your bones bubbling, eh?, in their dull stew and gets you to your feet? And answer me back? Now: nothing I have done has ever made me feel that anyone is better than I am. Though I was brought up to believe the reverse. See if Dionisio's still with my father. Why is it that of what they call the five Hindu hindrances you have only one: sloth? I have all the other four, craving, ill will, perplexity and restless brooding? I think that's right? Yes.

TIZON: They're still talking together.

LEONIDO: I could do with your sloth. Talking dowries and property and being important over my sister's body and disposing of it—as they think. So they think.

TIZON: If you have betrayed *Marcela's* virtue, you must keep it to yourself.

LEONIDO: You're as full of ifs as you are fleas. I've a harsh heart, Tizon, but don't sidle up to it or walk backwards away from it like my father does. That numb old nag now—he never took a difficult fence in his life either.

TIZON: He's an old man.

LEONIDO: He was born an old man. So was Dionisio. And you. All born dotards, and over-armoured. You need no protection from me.

TIZON: Need but not expect.

LEONIDO: Good. Don't expect. As for Marcela, she is the best part of the world for me. But she's not virtuous. No, not virtuous.

TIZON : She isn't now.

LEONIDO : She never was. I don't know what virtue is. Can you tell me? I have never had any myself and I never observed any in others either. You've none.

TIZON : You don't mean this.

LEONIDO : I *have* watched myself for signs of it, I promise you. I am purblind to the needs of others just as they are to mine. Your laughter may be my pleasure but your howlings might be too. I've set traps and tried to catch myself out in a virtuous act, but I've never done what people call a good thing that didn't give me pleasure. What ill-service can I do myself? What affection have I ever felt that didn't run home back to me at the end of the day? *Who* do I like? Or love? No one. Myself? A little. But not much, I'm not much lovable. Although I *am* preferable to anyone that is. For me I detest clever men and dullards I could roast and baste them slowly myself and read a book at the same time or top and tail a virgin. Or something. Simple men are too content and ambitious men are ambitious and ambitions too simple to be tolerated, tolerated or countenanced by *anyone*—at least who has ever sat down quietly and consistently and decently schooled themselves in pain. For their own pleasure? Well—there's more mettle in painful pleasure even than, than the restraints of over-protected and feeble men like them— those two there. You see, there, it all flies back to *pleasure*, like stooping falcon. Pleasure in self, shallow self, cracked and wormy as I may be. You're the same, Tizon. Surprised. We're no different, you and I. I *am* somewhat swifter at the kill. Always and every time. Will be. And forever more. There is no disinterest in nature. And good and evil are men's opinions of themselves.

TIZON: Dionisio's leaving.

LEONIDO: Good. *Why* do you watch me, Tizon?

TIZON: I am your servant.

LEONIDO: Can you, can you tell me the truth?

TIZON: I try.

LEONIDO: How can you be honest? You are cursed with dishonest eyes. Yes. It should be a handicap in a servant, but! Dare say it gets overlooked. Not noticed. They're full of blood, as usual. Have you looked at them? Poor pink, pink, not red, mark you pink lines. And meanness and envy, envy most of all. The will to wound but no will, lackey's eyes, traced indelicately, not attractively. Loaded with shame, shame and the dread of punishment. . . . No wonder I avoid your eyes. Why do you watch me?

TIZON: No servant tells the truth.

LEONIDO: Right! Nor could. Is the old man gone to bed?

TIZON: Yes.

LEONIDO: Very well. I think then . . . I shall go up to my sister. Well? Servant. Were you about to say something?

TIZON: No, my lord.

LEONIDO: My lord again. And what will *you* do while I am awake upstairs? Niffy dormouse?

TIZON: I shall wait.

LEONIDO: Not doze?

TIZON: No.

21

LEONIDO: No? Dozy?

TIZON: No.

LEONIDO: You'll doze. One day you *shall*. And who knows when that is? And perhaps you'll want to then? However . . . wait. You may get some more pleasure from me before then. So my sister's waiting. . . . Her light burns. Not over brightly but it burns. Just about to put it out . . . but I'll be there before then. Sisters are there to be trapped, Tizon. Tripped up. And over she goes. We'll talk again soon? I doubt I'll be sleeping much tonight, or if I do, something will waken me. Try not to doze. *He goes.* TIZON *stays awake.*

# ACT ONE

## Scene 2

MARCELA's *bedchamber.* MARCELA *in her nightgown with her* MAID. *The* MAID *looks out of the window.*

MAID : He's gone.

MARCELA : Who?

*Enter* LEONIDO.

LEONIDO : Why, Dionisio.

MAID : My lord!

LEONIDO : Gone. And so may you be now. Get along.

MAID : My lady is about to sleep.

LEONIDO : My lady is about to talk.

MAID : Sir!

LEONIDO : With me! We are not strangers to one another. You must know that there's a matter of blood between us. And between *us*? Please : the door.

MAID : Goodnight, lady!

*He thrusts her out.*

LEONIDO : Goodnight. And how *is* my lady then?

MARCELA : Prepared for sleep.

LEONIDO : Well, prepare yourself for bed first. All this sleeping. Your betrothed has gone off—to sleep too, no doubt.

MARCELA : I would rather you did not bawl up at my window.

LEONIDO : Bawl?

MARCELA : Ay! Bawl! Bridal bait!

LEONIDO : Bridal bait! This is your brother, chicken. Come along! Look at me now. What is it?

Aren't I allowed to bait you?

MARCELA: Leave me.

LEONIDO: Make me.

MARCELA: You bait to kill.

LEONIDO: Not you.

MARCELA: Yes. Me. You were never playful.

LEONIDO: I have played with you, Marcela, since the day
you were born.

MARCELA: To win or wound. Which you always do.

LEONIDO: How did you leave your betrothed?

MARCELA: Well.

LEONIDO: And easily?

MARCELA: He's angry with you.

LEONIDO: I may sleep tonight yet. The thought of
Dionisio's anger would make an owl yawn.
Well?

MARCELA: He complains you have lied all over Sicily that
he's a bastard. That his mother was a whore
and a crone and the only woman who has
died in childbed of old age.

LEONIDO: Does this sound like my invention?

MARCELA: Yes.

LEONIDO: There! It made you smile.

MARCELA: Well: He has not the edge himself to make
such a fancy, I admit.

LEONIDO: I may have said something.

MARCELA: Something? What was it?

LEONIDO: I don't know. About old bitches dropping
runts only. But bastard no. Dionisio is
*legitimate*. He's lawful as an endless sermon.
That's not to say proceedings shouldn't be
taken up against him for being born at all.
No, for certain he is in the common run of
legitimacy. A bastard's common too, but a

bastard you see's separate, a weed, often
strong, quite powerful. Like your
Charlemagne, your King Arthur, your
Gawain, your Roland and your Irish kings.
There! You're smiling at me. It *is* fun, not
repentance makes remission of sins.

MARCELA : There's none of either in you. Or ever will be.
*He mauls her.*
Go to your own bed, Leonido! You are mad.

LEONIDO : This is one of my lucid patches.
*They kiss. She stops struggling.*

MARCELA : Stop! You have a tongue like a lizard.

LEONIDO : There are a great many flies in your gullet.
They should be got out. Otherwise you will
choke.
*He kisses her again.*

MARCELA : Blow out the light . . . that's better.

LEONIDO : Now you're close to me again, Marcela.
Marcela. . . . When you look coldly on me, I
think my bowels will break. . . . Marcela
. . . Marcela. . . .

MARCELA : Yes?

LEONIDO : I can't see your face. . . . What defect is there
in me? I find beauty and comfort . . . and
sustenance . . . only . . . in you. There's no
light from the sea tonight. I can't see your
face. I don't care what people may speculate.
I do *not* want them to know. Not words or
movements or moments. Those are for our
pleasure, only. Marcela? Secrecy *is* the nerve
of love. Can you see me? Marcela? Are you
asleep? . . .

25

# ACT ONE

## Scene 3

GERARDO's *garden.* DIONISIO *sits with his bride,* MARCELA, *on the terrace by the sea.* TIZON *lies drunk among the flowers. Enter* GERARDO *with* LEONIDO, *who kicks* TIZON *as he passes.*

GERARDO: I cannot understand you.

LEONIDO: Or young men like me.

GERARDO: Or young men like you.

LEONIDO: Whoever *they* may be. Only old men seem to have the good fortune to meet them.

GERARDO: What?

LEONIDO: Go on, father, you talk endless doggerel as if it were the poetry of revealed doctrine. But go on. It's your privilege.

GERARDO: *You* are too privileged. In my time——

LEONIDO: As if now wasn't his time——

GERARDO: —time it was all war and uncertainty. Now everything is easy come by and you and those like you hang about sniffing blood ungratefully and harrying everyone and everything in your rancorousness.

LEONIDO: Old men inhabit what are clear for miles as fortresses all their lives and talk as if they were pigging it in mud huts.

GERARDO: What?

LEONIDO: There's no cutting a way through your hairy old ear. Is there? I say that clapper tongue of yours has deafened you inside that hollow

26

bell. Hollow bell.

GERARDO: Bell. Wedding bell?

LEONIDO: Bedding well. Yes. Very soon from the look of them. Your head, father, the top, there, where your cap screws on, you rancid old jar.

GERARDO: You are too full of contempt.

LEONIDO: I take in a fresh stock twice weekly and whenever I am with *you*.

GERARDO: Do you hear?

LEONIDO: Alas, my ears are *not* overgrown with old man's moss. Could you not clean up that old garden to your brain one day, father? It might not be easier to enter but it might be more pleasant for the rest of us.

GERARDO: You tread upon your sister's bridal gown. You abuse her husband. You hiss dislike and envy at the priest. I think your midriff and your backbone must be full of—serpents.

LEONIDO: They'd be useful worms for dim dogs like the priest—or, indeed, you, father. I say! At least, they stop me growing fat on commonplaces.

GERARDO: See, there. Look there. Your sister still weeps at the remembrance of your cruelty. All her days, I dare say. And on her wedding day.

LEONIDO: Or at the yawning expectation of her wedding night. Or the expectation of her yawning wedding night. Tizon? What? Retiring already, Marcela!

MARCELA: I am tired and unwell.

LEONIDO: Who has made you unwell then? Dionisio?

DIONISIO: You shall not come near her again, Leonido. I have told her. Nor enter our house ever.

LEONIDO: Not welcome? Nowhere? Marcela?

MARCELA: Nowhere.

LEONIDO: Never?

MARCELA: No.

GERARDO: Come, child. Take her to bed, Dionisio. It's
best. Your brother has not altogether blighted
this day for you, and thank heavens, the night
is not in his hands. My blessings on you both
and be at peace together while you may. And
remember Father Augustine.

MARCELA: "Our heart is restless till it finds itself in
thee."

GERARDO: Good, child. Take her, Dionisio.

LEONIDO: Why you've been busy, bride, you've been
gospelling and swapping pieties with the priest.

MARCELA: We prayed together.

DIONISIO: All night.

LEONIDO: You'll not be up so long, so don't hurry. So!
This is why you are so feverish—from sitting
out in a devotional draught. That's why her
bed was empty!

MARCELA: I was not seeking your permission. And,
Leonido, listen from this time: I obey only
my husband.

GERARDO: There, Leonido. Embrace it, and off with you.

MARCELA: Goodnight, father.

GERARDO: Goodnight, my child.
*They turn.*

LEONIDO: Marcela? (*Pause.*) Goodnight.
*She stares coldly, grasps* DIONISIO's *hand and
goes into the house.* GERARDO *regards him for a
moment, then follows them. Music.* LEONIDO
*stands stricken. Presently,* TIZON *hands him a
flagon of wine to drink from.* LEONIDO *takes it
and drinks.*

So. Rome has spoken. The matter is settled.

28

TIZON : That's the way of it, my lord. That's the way of it.

LEONIDO : What's the way of what? Must you look out at the sea and not here? There's nothing stirring out there.

TIZON : Quietly, my lord. They are joined together now——

LEONIDO : And by what dishonest mortar.

TIZON : You must accept it.

LEONIDO : I accept nothing. Nothing is offered.

TIZON : Her light is on.

LEONIDO : Not for me . . . it isn't . . . being looked on as a good bargain . . . Gerardo! Do you hear me now! I always worked for passion rather than for profit, for the salt pearls that ran down the knots of her spine. Marcela!

*He stares up at* MARCELA's *window. More music.* TIZON *drops off.* LEONIDO *draws his sword. He strikes him with it.* TIZON *is brought to his feet by the sudden pain.*

LEONIDO : Draw! Draw!

*Confused,* TIZON *does so.*

*They duel.* LEONIDO's *rage helps him to beat* TIZON *quickly and he has his sword pointing at his belly.*

There!

TIZON *goes.*

One day, one day of your lifetime I shall kill you with this sword. Now? No. Tonight or tomorrow or in a year. Whenever you affront me most or I'm most impatient. Don't misjudge the time by my mood. It may be when I'm gasping for want of enemies or running idly up to a joke. . . . See how alert

29

you must be! You'd better keep awake while you can. After all, that alone, that incessant discipline, will add to your span. It must do so. Now, isn't that a fierce, energetic structure for a man to be alive in. That'll keep you awake. It'll keep you *occupied*. You won't *dare* sleep. Or perhaps you will. We'll see. It may not matter to you, it may come, it may not. Now you're breathing, now you're bleeding. Ah! *Never* turn your back on me. Or look away. *Watch* me, Tizon. And now I shall spoil the bride's sleep. You may as well wait a while. Relax yourself a little.

*He takes a lamp and goes, leaving* TIZON *to wipe the blood from his face.*

# ACT ONE

## SCENE 4

MARCELA's *bedchamber. Enter* LEONIDO *with lamp.*
MARCELA *in bed.*

MARCELA: Dionisio?

LEONIDO: No—Leonido!

MARCELA: I beg you to leave me. Brother, you have had
the best of me.

LEONIDO: And you of me.

MARCELA: Well! Now leave the rest to Dionisio. It's little
enough but the best for all of us.

LEONIDO: At last! You confess it was the best!

MARCELA: I confess it to flatter you, to be rid of you
before my husband returns.

LEONIDO: Are you so hot for this husband's—*hus*band—
husband's jobbery? Is there no more,
sweetheart? Please?

MARCELA: Ask me no explanations. There is no more. I
have nothing for you.

LEONIDO: Marcela. We have been conspirators. Can you
deny it? We have never thought of winning—
only of each other. I thought of us only as
two children together.
*She laughs.*
Anything, any excess is preferable to this
miserable subordination, this imposture,
this——

MARCELA: Go!

LEONIDO: This low,—low, uterine appeasement!

31

MARCELA: Dionisio!

LEONIDO: It is only in you that I see a foot ahead of me
and my heartbeat recovers. What is it now?
A life of scavenging for slops of your
attention. Eh? Upturned from the window to
your bedchamber? Remember, my mouth, my
mouth, your mouth, Marcela.

MARCELA: A man cannot make a wife of his sister. It's
bane for both of them. Don't ask me why.
Ask the world or God, or what, but there's
law and nature against you in their battalions.
Now go, my dear, I am afraid enough already.

LEONIDO: Marcela, I am a woman's son. Your mother's
son. I love women. Shall I *tell* you? No? Why?
Sister: when did you ever look for me as I
looked for you?

MARCELA: Always.
*They kiss.*
Dionisio! He's coming!

LEONIDO: Sister, what has this man done . . . to you?
He has laid his mark on you. You are healed
somehow and hardened. Where's your blood
now? Your lap is as wooden as a bench. You
*will* not, no, *not*, sweetheart, not deprive me?
Take off your shift. . . .
LEONIDO *begins stripping* MARCELA, *who
screams.*
DIONISIO *enters.*

MARCELA: Dionisio! My God, *help* me!
*The men duel.* DIONISIO *falls.* LEONIDO *strikes*
MARCELA *with his sword and goes.* MARCELA
*goes to* DIONISIO *as he recovers.*

32

# ACT ONE

## SCENE 5

GERARDO's *garden. Enter* LEONIDO *with bloody sword. He grins at* TIZON.

LEONIDO: It's done.

TIZON: But not well. Was it?

LEONIDO: No, not well this time, but let's say we celebrated all the occasions past when it *was* well done.

TIZON: Have you no feeling? Even for reckoning?

LEONIDO: I have God's credit for the moment. Let him settle up for me, and send in his account when he wants to. He must know my credit's good, indeed. He has never—in his eternal life—had a client with better prospects or security. Nor ever will have. Come. I'm bored here. Let's go.

TIZON: Where?

LEONIDO: We'll have a late stroll in the market place. You'll enjoy that. And you will sleep all the better for it.

TIZON: You want to show off your sister's blood in the market place.

LEONIDO: Oh, you think I killed her?

TIZON: Didn't you?

LEONIDO: No. I added a few grace notes to her face.

TIZON: God gave her one face and a good one, and you add to it! Like mine. Don't you think you'll pay for all this handiwork of yours.

C                                   33

LEONIDO : I'll tell you : send the bill in to God. I'll settle
with him later. Don't concern yourself, Tizon.
You'll lose your sleep.

TIZON : For the final settling up! I will stay awake. I
promise you.

LEONIDO : Good, Tizon. I do believe I've smoked out
your torpor. For tonight run! With me!
Come! Here's the old man with the other. Oh
—breathless with survival too.

*They hide. Enter* GERARDO *and* DIONISIO.
Nasty palaverer. He's woken the old pudding
from his prayers.

DIONISIO : How can I tell you?

LEONIDO : How indeed?

DIONISIO : I came upon them together. Together, my
wife, his sister and both of them your
children. It's quite famous the kind of man he
is, but I thought I was secure on this occasion.
But I was wrong. Señor. I blame you. Yes,
you. You have not checked him as you could
have done and now we all suffer for it. He has
stolen from us all, from you, from his sister,
and now from me. Look at my face!

GERARDO : Marcela. Did she defend herself?

DIONISIO : As well as she could. And now she has a
striped face like mine to show for it.

GERARDO : Oh, Leonido!

DIONISIO : Nothing will change him. I shall hunt him
down.

LEONIDO *appears.*

LEONIDO : Hunt me down then.

GERARDO : What have you done with my daughter?

DIONISIO : Not what he set out for.

LEONIDO : Not on *this* evening. However : it is true I

34

have left some equipment somewhere—
sometime—in that particular warren.

DIONISIO *draws*.

It is true, father, I tried to rob her—honour
on this special night. Not because she wanted
me to but because that is how *I* was born. By
the same brutality. As you well know. With
any good fortune I shall still insult her blood
and yours too and take away what little
honour you have creasing beneath your
mattress. I did it not because it was good but
interesting. I am glad to see it's painful to
both of you.

GERARDO: Leonido. Why must you do these things to us?
You are pillaging my heart. For all his mercy,
the good God must punish you with the
miseries of hell. Oh, if I could be wrong in
that.

LEONIDO: Then be comforted. The precedents for your
prognostications are most encouraging.

DIONISIO *lunges at* LEONIDO.

Out of the way, old man.

GERARDO: You call me old man because you have
darkened the name father. Because you know
you deserve no father nor even to mouth the
word.

LEONIDO: So! You want my attention!

*He strikes him.* GERARDO *cries out.*

DIONISIO: Father, you'll be revenged.

LEONIDO: If I fix a place, will you trust me?

DIONISIO: Yes, even you.

LEONIDO: You must not expect more or better of me. . . .
My fingers are like quills. Read the message
on your face. . . . Very well. I can't bear to

35

look on that any longer. If it's revenge then, let us say sunset. By the seashore. Tonight.
*He goes.*

GERARDO: Humble him, oh God! I am too infirm. Let some Moorish lance skewer my own son. May they drag him on a halter into Tunis, a bruised litter of flesh strung behind some fleeing camel!

DIONISIO: Be calm, father. You have a new son here. In me. Take a little pleasure in your son and daughter and what's to come from both of them. Let me lift you. There. On my shoulder. There.

GERARDO: Let's go to see your wife, my daughter. Your grief is mine just as she is mine.

DIONISIO: There, father. Come.

GERARDO: Let the world judge these two men. I ask no more of it. Nothing.

# ACT ONE

## SCENE 6

*Sicily. A beach.* LEONIDO *lies sleeping. Enter* KING
BERLEBEYO, ZULEMA *and* ZARRABULLI.

KING: Praise Allah. Sicilian sand! Feel it.

ZULEMA: As you commanded, oh King.

ZARRAB.: We can snare all the Christians we can carry
home here, and then back off to Tunis.

KING: I wish they'd appear. If it were not for Lidora,
I'd be at home. Where are we?

ZULEMA: This is the port of Alicarte. And this is the
beach of Saso. Christians come here, I promise
you, my king.

ZARRAB.: Take care you are not converted. They are
great wheedlers.

ZULEMA: Here's one: he's asleep.

KING: Take his sword.

ZULEMA: Ah!

*He takes it.*

KING: Now wake him.

LEONIDO: Why, you black lard!

KING: Tie his hands.

LEONIDO: I can see, sir, you have not been to Sicily
before. Here then.

*He grabs branch from a tree.*

KING: *Kill* him, Zulema! Kill the Christian!

LEONIDO: Kill the Christian! Kill the Moor!

*They fight.* LEONIDO *fights like a madman and
disarms them all.*

37

KING : I surrender! Surrender! I never, anywhere, saw
such strength. I am your slave, and if it is your
pleasure, I think it will be mine. Who are you?

LEONIDO : I will tell you. But drink this wine first.

KING : I don't drink wine.

LEONIDO : Drink : King.

*He drinks.*

Well, Moor. King Berlebeyo, oh, I know you.
I was born in Alicarte, by the river Saso near
the mountains of Petralia. They say that when
my mother gave birth to me, the whole island
heard it and her breasts were covered in blood,
as a sign of hatred, you see, and Etna, yes,
Etna erupted, and the only contented soul here
was my own. They were frightened of me from
the first. Not that I killed anyone. Only
wished to. They were all consumed with
process. Had no idea of the unique. Me, I had
an overstrong instinct, you understand and this
is an island of over protected people. The
range of possibilities in living here shrinks
with every year. Soon, it will be every week,
then daily. I am a liar. Lying is inescapable to
me. I understand a liar and I cherish a thief. I
think I have raped thirty women and I don't
include my mother, who hardly resisted. My
sister took to it regularly and easily except on
her wedding night. Why I don't know.
Something is wrong. God or myself. But then :
I stabbed her twice in the face, oh yes, and her
husband. I could fatten *him* up for you. And
then there was the man who calls himself my
father, but no more, I dare say. That pleased
me more than all the rest. So, you see, proud

38

Moor, *you* are the tail end.

KING : Valiant and noble Leonido, by the sacred
temple where lies the holy and divine body of
Mahomet, although I am ashamed of capture
and am heir to a Kingdom, I rejoice in being
your captive. I come here to please a Moorish
lady whom I long for. Her name is Lidora and
she asked me for a Sicilian Christian, even
though she has more than she knows what to
do with. So I come. And found my master.

LEONIDO : Then we shall take you back to Lidora, eh?
All of us. Drink. Go on.

KING : If I do—Mahomet will punish me.

LEONIDO : Refer him—to me.
*He drinks.*
There—we shall get on. Now : give me a cloak
and turban.
*Enter* TIZON. *He watches in horror.*
Ah, Tizon. Help me with these.

ZARRAB. : Master! It is *my* task.
ZARRABULLI *and* ZULEMA *robe him in Moorish
costume. The others watch.*

LEONIDO : What do you think, Tizon?
*He lunges.*
Dozing, Tizon! Do I make a good Moor?
When do you think you'll die?

TIZON : You make a grand Turk. A Suliman——

LEONIDO : Go and tell my father this—I renounce his
blood. Also his God, his law, the baptism and
the sacraments, oh yes, and the Passion and
Death. I think I shall follow Mahomet.

TIZON : Leonido! How can you ask me? I dare not
take such a message.

LEONIDO : Dare not! Well, then——

TIZON: No—I'll take it.

LEONIDO: Yes.

KING: May you wear this and live forever, Leonido!

LEONIDO: And you too. And now let us go and see this Lidora.

KING: I am your slave.

LEONIDO: And my master.

TIZON: I will go then. Think on this, Leonido.

LEONIDO: I don't think. But I shall observe my processes as well as I can.

TIZON: I'll take this long cloak of yours and hat as witnesses of what's happened. Remember: you have a debt to pay to heaven.

LEONIDO: And remember also: I have the best bond. Let the Good Lord pay pound for pound. I'll settle later.

*Exit.*

# ACT TWO

## SCENE 1

*Tunis. Enter* LEONIDO *in Moorish costume. With him* LIDORA, *a Moorish lady.*

LIDORA: Stop.

LEONIDO: Why?

LIDORA: Turn and face me.

LEONIDO: But I've no wish to face you.

LIDORA: You are cruel.

LEONIDO: It comes easily if you apply yourself to it.

LIDORA: I love you.

LEONIDO: Me?

LIDORA: You.

LEONIDO: Or my cruelty is it? What if I'm not for the asking?

LIDORA: I shall die.

LEONIDO: Now or later?

LIDORA: On your account.

LEONIDO: So you keep saying.

LIDORA: Great Argolan!

LEONIDO: Lidora?

LIDORA: Won't you love me?

LEONIDO: I've no need, nor the energy or curiosity.

LIDORA: Oh, you are cruel.

LEONIDO: Yes, and you're a fool. I am only one of them but you can be both.

LIDORA: Dearest!

LEONIDO: I am weary of your Moorish yapping and haggling. Now leave me.

LIDORA : Does my beauty mean nothing to you?

LEONIDO : The sun hasn't burned up my head even if it has yours. To me : you are no more beautiful than some overheated whelp trailing strangers in the bazaar. I have loved oh, many women, Lidora, or performed, I suppose, the rituals of it passably well. I allow then that you're beautiful and you can take some pride in that, though not much. Beauty is just one of many wells you might have been dropped in when your mother bore you. And all Moorish women bore me. Oh, there's a great deal of display in you, but I think it promises too much. There's a trick in there, possibly hundreds of them, and that, Lidora, is repellent. To me.

LIDORA : I am Moorish but I too hate Moors. I have much to give you. I know it. Love me, Argolan.

*Enter the* KING.

KING : Is this how you observe the King's law?

LIDORA : When did I not heed your law?

KING : Why, by trying to enlist proud Argolan here as one of your lovers. Now.

LIDORA : What offence is there in that then?

KING : There is this offence : you swore that when I brought you a Christian you would love me.

LIDORA : True. But you are not betrayed yet. Besides, for all that, what Christian did you bring back? You brought back a *Moor* and I am in love with him. I would give him my heart's blood if he asked for it.

LEONIDO : Don't be rash, Lidora. Heart's blood adds relish to a dull, many a dull dish.

42

LIDORA: I would give him more than relish. I love him
even for the clothes he wears and his
renunciation. If he were still Christian I
should love him.
*Exit.*

KING: Well, Argolan. What do you say?

LEONIDO: It's a common pattern. The more she protests,
the less I want to hear about it. When I love
this woman, Mahomet will no longer be a
holy prophet, Berlebeyo.

KING: For this favour you are doing me, Argolan,
you shall see the true art and scope of the
great love I bear for you. Tunis is yours.
Demand whatever you want of it. My
Kingdom is yours.

LEONIDO: I don't want someone else's Kingdom.

KING: Try on my crown.

LEONIDO: I'll not go shares. *If* I wear your crown one
day, it shall be in my own Kingdom.

KING: Are you mad? Remember: you have left your
own homeland behind.

LEONIDO: A sprightly old cock will crow anywhere he
likes. Call on your government, King. Call on
your city. Call out Mahomet. I am going to
eat you! Out, Moor, out with your sword!

KING: Lidora!
*Enter* LIDORA.

LIDORA: What's this?

LEONIDO: The one you love. I shall bust your law, break
your city, strike at friendship and kill your
King. I'll wait for you by the river.
*Exit.*

KING: Rot you, you dog!

LIDORA: Wait. Wait, noble Berlebeyo. Check yourself.

KING : What?

LIDORA : Swallow your bitterness. It's acid that runs through dwarfs. For the love of me, and yourself, pardon him.

KING : If you wish it. But only then, then I will. I cannot see for anger, nor can I now, only you and your love can rein me in. Hold me in. Hold me. There!

LIDORA : May Mahomet strengthen you forever.

*Enter* ZARRABULLI.

ZARRAB. : Lidora, what is the reward for good news?

KING : Bargains after.

LIDORA : Tell us.

ZARRAB. : Zulema is at the gates with as many Christian prisoners as you'd wish for.

LIDORA : Oh! Is it true?

ZARRAB. : They are Sicilians.

LIDORA : Tell him to come in.

ZARRAB. : He is very Pompey.

KING : He's a fine soldier.

*Enter* ZULEMA, GERARDO, TIZON *and* MARCELA *—prisoners*.

ZULEMA : Come in, Christians. Kiss King Berlebeyo's feet. And you, my lord, put your foot in their mouths. And in mine.

LIDORA : Oh, you have excelled yourself! Tell me what has happened.

ZULEMA : I have been lucky, as you shall see.

LIDORA : Tell me.

ZULEMA : Lidora, I set out happily from Tunis, with no thought but of your pleasure, with a hundred Moors. After weeks on the water, I made out the high walls of Sicily, packed with those people who follow this cross, followers of the

44

naked prophet, who they say is on nodding
terms with God. I landed, split my men into
bands and looked for the quarry. In the
darkness we saw nothing, but at dawn on the
foreshore Allah rewarded us for the night
with three men and one woman. One of the
men I spliced with my cutlass to clear the air
and the remainder are here before you. Three
fine Sicilians for your pleasure.

LIDORA: You have pleased me so much, so exceedingly,
I can think of only one gift adequate.

ZULEMA: Lidora: you offer me more than any conquest
I have ever made.

LIDORA: You're worthy of it.

KING: Divine Mahomet. Do you give yourself to
anyone for a gift.

ZULEMA: I think, great lord, *your* claim is undisputed.
Forgive me. Let Lidora keep this gift. I
remain your slave. I meant only to give you,
my lord, delight through her.

KING: She does not deserve Christians for servants
but Mahomet himself. Zulema, I present this
ring to you. Take it but not for payment. As
a sign of affection.

ZULEMA: On another expedition I will do better. For
you both. You shall have the Eastern church
on one hand, the Western on the other.
Roman and Eastern shall touch the soles of
your feet.

TIZON: So much talk and no wine with it, ever.

LIDORA: With your leave, lord, I'll send for Argolan.

KING: Wait till I have gone.

ZULEMA: Have you fallen out?

LIDORA: It is over now. Argolan is coming back to us.

ZULEMA: Then he can meet his countrymen.

KING: Find him.

ZULEMA: I shall go. I only wish to serve you.

LIDORA: I know how you should be repaid.

*He goes.*

KING: I will leave you alone. I've no fancy for any of these.

*He goes.*

LIDORA: What is the matter? Why are you weeping? Remember you don't yet know whose power you have fallen into. Even though you are prisoners, you must not look like this. Your face is beautiful. Let me look at it.

MARCELA: Oh noble and beautiful Moor. It is not for myself. What moves me is the condition of this old man. His dignity and wisdom are the world's luck. If I should serve you, it'll not matter. I know how to bear things, and I hope you will be patient with me. But how can this man serve you when he has such a short time to live. How, Señora, can he be of use when he is worn out. What pleasure can you take in these powdery bones? He is certain to displease and irritate. Punish me for his fault, I beg you, even twice as much. If the father errs, then let the daughter pay, Señora, let the daughter pay.

LIDORA: No more. Now I beg *you*. Wipe your eyes. What is your name?

MARCELA: Marcela.

LIDORA: Calm yourself, Marcela. Your father may be a prisoner, but he has found another daughter.

MARCELA: Señora.

LIDORA: Old man. Embrace me, old man.

46

GERARDO *weeps*.

Our love is clasped in this for good. Hold me closer. Ask him for me, Marcela, for he will listen to you. Even if all Tunis rises up, I will affirm today that I have met my father. Are you happy to be father to me?

GERARDO : I will be your slave.

LIDORA : Put up a front before the Moors and lift your head a little. Stop crying, Marcela. We are sisters. Truly.

TIZON : What about me? Who lifts my head for me?
*Enter* LEONIDO.

LEONIDO : Well? Ah Tizon! You have woken in a strange place.

LIDORA : I wanted only to please you, Argolan.

LEONIDO : And I wished to please you. So?

MARCELA : Dear God, what have I done to you to set me under him again!

LIDORA : I wanted to show how much I adore you, Argolan. These prisoners, all Christians, have just been given to me by Zulema. They all serve me, and I want you to know, they will serve you with me.
GERARDO *goes to kiss the sole of* LEONIDO'*s feet*.
May it please Allah!

LEONIDO : I will treat you all as you deserve. Are you honoured to be at my feet? Heaven casts you down just as it casts me up. You at my feet, yes, you paltry old toad. I'll not have your mouth near any shoe of mine, or I'll have to burn it afterwards. Get up! You're a brave groveller. Own the earth do you? Do you?
*He kicks* GERARDO *in the mouth*.

47

Get up!

GERARDO: Oh, divine heaven!

TIZON: You struck him on his knees.

LEONIDO: Why not. It's his natural posture.

GERARDO: This is what a good father suffers from a bad son.

LIDORA: Father, get up, get up. I put myself in your hands. What is happening between you?

GERARDO: Oh, bad son.

LEONIDO: I your son? Utter the name son again to me and I'll hook your jaw to the rafters.

LIDORA: What have I done to you, Leonido?

LEONIDO: Do you know me?

MARCELA: I never knew you! Why don't you kill me— Moor?

LEONIDO: Mahomet will have his vengeance on you both. You won't find protection here.

LIDORA: Father, sit down, sit down in this chair.

MARCELA: *Moor*, do as you like. Do as you like.

LEONIDO: Oh, Marcela. I've waited for you.

MARCELA: But take care.

LIDORA: Come to my arms, Señor.

GERARDO: Do not weep, child. I am better.
*Sits.*

MARCELA: Take care, Leonido.
LEONIDO *takes out his dagger.*

LEONIDO: Father? Father?

GERARDO: Yes?

LEONIDO: Do your old eyes see this?

GERARDO: They do.

LEONIDO: Then they still see very well.
*He strikes* GERARDO *in the eyes.* GERARDO *covers them with a cloth.*

MARCELA: Lidora, hold him!

LEONIDO: Now you can see less than you ever chose to see.

LIDORA: What jungle did you spring from. Oh!

LEONIDO: Kiss this blade, old man. Down, go on! Your daughter wants me to kill you in her own way. Marcela, do your duty by me. Yes? Or watch the old toad croak.

MARCELA: There's no answering you. I can't.

GERARDO: Don't be doubtful, Marcela. Better that I should die than you should be his lover.

LEONIDO: Does either matter?

GERARDO: I will not have her dishonoured.

LEONIDO: Answer?

MARCELA: Kill him.

LEONIDO: So!

MARCELA: Wait!

GERARDO: Don't lose heart, daughter.

LEONIDO: He'd best die. I assure you.

MARCELA: Die then! No!

LEONIDO: Speak up, sister.

MARCELA: I want him to die.

LEONIDO: Ah!

MARCELA: Not to die!

LEONIDO: You're in some difficulty?

*She covers her eyes but* LEONIDO *makes her watch.*

Now!

MARCELA: Now?

LEONIDO: And on your daughter's head!

GERARDO: Follow him, Marcela. Follow him.

MARCELA: Then do it.

LEONIDO: Do it?

MARCELA: Yes.

LIDORA: Argolan!

*She holds him back.*
LEONIDO : By the Koran, Argolan will have you for
dessert. But Tunis shall burn first. TUNIS
FIRST.
*He goes.*

# ACT TWO

## SCENE 2

*Tunis. Enter* LEONIDO, *distracted, like a madman. A voice interrupts now and then as he speaks.*

LEONIDO: Marcela!

VOICE: Lidora.

LEONIDO: Marcela. I feel the bond tightening. Yes, it's tightening.

VOICE: Calm.

LEONIDO: Beyond logic so beyond doubt. Marcela, miserable, deluded and deluding family. Where are you? Where's your timorous Dionisio? Where is your *memory* of me? It shall soon fail. My imprint will have died out of all hearts inside a month. Discard. A discard. I have been mostly, a fair mixture of intelligence, mostly, self-criticism and, yes, gullibility. Yes, that's a hesitating assessment.

VOICE: Hesitate.

LEONIDO: But there's a hint in it.

VOICE: Hint.

LEONIDO: Allah! God! Marcela. Gullibility, self-criticism. Such people are always identifying, scrabbling for their stars, for signs in themselves, in the latest philosophy twice a week. If you have no dreams or portents for the day, they will knock one up for you. If you have not hit your wife or thought of killing your father. Mother. Daughter. Son.

51

They will think you impoverished, or
insensible. You will be made to dream again.
I want no more dreams.

VOICE: For that which I do.

LEONIDO: I allow not. For what I would, that I do not.
But what I hate: that I do. I know that in me.

VOICE: In my flesh.

LEONIDO: There is no good thing. For the will is present
in me. But how to perform what is good. I
find. . . .

VOICE: Not.

LEONIDO: For the good thing I would, I do not. . . . But
the evil: that I do. So then I find the law.
When I do good evil is present in me. For I
delight in the law of God after the inward
man. But I see another law in my members,
warring against the law of my mind, and
bringing me into captivity.

VOICE: To the law of sin.

LEONIDO: Which of my members? Who shall deliver me?
*Enter* SHEPHERD *barefoot.*

SHEPHERD: Cannot a hard heart soften?

LEONIDO: Ay, soften. That will do. Soften is the course.

SHEPHERD: Curse.

LEONIDO: It's you. You, who spoke. Who are you?

SHEPHERD: I am a shepherd.

LEONIDO: Where are you going?

SHEPHERD: Doing shepherd's work.

LEONIDO: What are sheep to you? Or you to sheep even?
Leave them. Let them die as they want to.

SHEPHERD: No. As I want.

LEONIDO: Have you called out?

SHEPHERD: It won't hear.

LEONIDO: Not?

SHEPHERD : So I grieve for it.

LEONIDO : You don't look like grief. Give up.

SHEPHERD : It was too costly for me. I am afraid he shall die.

LEONIDO : Who shall die?

SHEPHERD : Why, the sheep.

LEONIDO : Damn your ignorant sheep! What are you? A Moor?

SHEPHERD : I am no Moor.

LEONIDO : You have the look of one. They are the mercenaries of Allah. They are all cut throats, and stall holders with prayers on their lips and all the time graft at their elbow.

SHEPHERD : *You* are dressed as a Moor.

LEONIDO : I was once dressed as a Sicilian. Christian. But neither Sicilian nor Christian meant anything to me. Who are you? Why are you loitering? What do you want? Alms? Go away.

SHEPHERD : I want no alms. But the debt you owe must be recovered.

LEONIDO : Perhaps you are a thief. I am a thief myself and I know the signs of a thief. Just as I know a liar. Go away, lunatic.

SHEPHERD : In this meagre pouch is what you owe me.

LEONIDO : Give it to me. I'll look at it. But let me warn you: if you are making game of me, I shall kill you.

SHEPHERD : I hear you.
*Hands him the pouch.*

LEONIDO : I can hardly hold it.

SHEPHERD : It is harder still to carry.

LEONIDO : Ah, a conjurer's bag. I knew you had a look of the bazaar about you. Let's look inside.

First dip: there's a lucky one. A crown. I shall
wear that. It will look better on me. I feel
calmer. Emptying this loon's pouch, perhaps.
Oh, delightful! A tunic. Oh yes. And with lash
marks on it. It looks like a motto, is it your
motto, some device? Are the lashes my motto?
Why? Do you think I'm a slave? Like you?
What else is there? A rope. That's good. I may
lash you with this. So this is your bond. What
are these things? More clothes.

*He takes out a cross.*

Why are you mocking me? If you were God
himself, you'd get no reprieve from me. I am
going to kill you.

*He falls to the ground.*

SHEPHERD: Why are you afraid, Leonido? Who are you
thinking of? Your mother? Gerardo?
Marcela?

LEONIDO: Marcela!

SHEPHERD: Think of your sister's body. Then look into
my heart. Think of your father's eyes. Then
look into mine. Tell me, Leonido, what are
you waiting for? What? Now that the debt is
due, what are you thinking of paying with?
Today, Leonido, I have to collect everything
you have spent. I paid for all of them, but this
is the reckoning. And I am here for it.

LEONIDO: I am overspent. It's not in your interest to
believe me. But it is the case. I always knew it
would be so. You will get, if you are so
fortunate, a bankrupt's farewell, which is
somewhat less than a penny in the pound. So
be it then. You will have had access to my
books, so there is nothing for me to do but

54

acknowledge each item, which might give
satisfaction to you as a kind of divine lawyer's
fee, but as wearisome to me as the hell I go to
and the hell I came from. You shall have my
life, which is what you came for. It's no more
than fluff at the bottom of the pocket.
*Gives him fluff.*
SHEPHERD: Let me embrace you.
LEONIDO: Kill me first.
*The* SHEPHERD *goes.*
I'll go to such extremes the world will use me
as an example. Let's off, first with the
scimitar. Cloak, hood. And turban. Tunic, yes,
better than the Moorish for a debtor of my
proportions. It's a good garment to stand trial
in. We don't expect acquittal do we? Perhaps
*they* do though. He looked uncertain. No, we
want a harsh tribunal and the full exercise of
justice. You, crown, you sit between my ears,
like a child above the crowd. Tears from ears,
tears from the heart, there's a wad of tears.
And rope, rope, you shall need me too. If I'm
to settle up. Be made to seem to settle up.
*Moves off. Blackout. Lights up. Enter* ZULEMA
*and the* KING.
KING: Know this, Zulema. Do not be surprised at
Leonido's reversal. A bad Christian was never
a good Moor. When he followed his own
heavenly father, he never kept his limits. Tunis
was no different to him. The man who jeers at
his three-for-one in God will gob in
Mahomet's eye for sixpence.
ZULEMA: There he is. What's he doing?
KING: Kneeling. Go on bind him.

55

ZULEMA: I will try.

LEONIDO: Come, Moor, come all of you. Leonido is no longer the same man, but he will flog you a little like he did before. And then you shall have me. You shall have your man, defeated as I am. The liar you found so difficult will become a dismal lamb.

*They fight. Brutally. Then* LEONIDO *throws in his hand.*

Now you may take me.

ZULEMA: It's a trick.

LEONIDO: No more than all the rest, Zulema. Come along, take this rope around my neck. Grab it, go on. I am a mule now. Or lamb or what you want of me. If you want pickings from Mahomet, here's one for you.

KING: Leave him to me, Zulema. *I* want the slaughtering of this butcher.

*Chase.* LEONIDO *laughs. Dances.*

Got him! Got! You!

*They bind him with the rope.*

Let's go. To Tunis.

LEONIDO: To Tunis. Christ support me!

*Blackout. Lights up.* LIDORA *and* TIZON.

LIDORA: Go on! You are so lethargic. I want to catch up.

TIZON: Yes, ah, the articles, well, you know those already.

LIDORA: And our Father and the Credo.

TIZON: The Ave Maria.

LIDORA: Go on! Go on!

TIZON: Listen then, Señora. I will teach you the precepts which we must observe if we are to enjoy God's favour.

56

LIDORA: How many are there?

TIZON: No more than ten.

LIDORA: Do you mean a Christian's salvation depends only on ten commandments?

TIZON: That's all.

LIDORA: Tell me what they are quickly. It seems a bargain. But first tell me again how he died. I am confused here. How can man be mortal and immortal at once? How can he die and yet have eternal life?

TIZON: You have grasped the spike of it. Listen: For the first sin which Adam committed against God, for eating the fruit of the world, we are all of us condemned without hope or remedy. Now, because this was a sin against immense God, immense, you see, only another immense being could atone for it. Being God, as he was immortally powerful, like his Father in heaven, he could not die. Could not.

LIDORA: Most interesting. And the next?

TIZON: The next? Well: so he took on the form of a human. Human form, you see.

LIDORA: Yes, I see.

TIZON: And then, being born of a virgin, he was better than any man. Naturally.

LIDORA: I see that.

TIZON: That is the Virgin Mary, well known where I come from, for the comfort of the afflicted, refuge of sinners and so on and so forth and what have you. She gave birth, you see, to this little fellow, in a most unsalubrious sort of place, and, well, there it is, in the end he was crucified and suffered as you heard in the Credo. Is that all?

57

LIDORA : Tell me, Tizon: shall *I* be able to see God?

TIZON : That's a difficult question as you'd appreciate, madam. No, I would say no. You are of mortal flesh and therefore I don't see how you could be expected to. None of us do. Do you have any wine? This talk makes me——

*Enter* GERARDO, DIONISIO *and* MARCELA.

MARCELA : Lidora! Lidora, my beloved husband. My husband Dionisio is back here among us!

LIDORA : Dionisio! Marcela, how is this?

DIONISIO : One day, Lidora, when your Tunisian troops came to Alicarte, God must have either wanted me to suffer or to be able to see you. My wife, her father, a servant and myself were walking by the shore when the Moors found us. They took the others and left me for dead in the sand. They took my wife from me and this old man, the most respected head in Alicarte. But it was heaven's wish, beautiful Moor, that I should recover, as you can see. Recover to find my father without sight and my wife all but blinded by what she has seen, what no one should see. It is a wicked reunion, I tell you, Moor.

LIDORA : I can think of nothing to say to comfort you. Tizon? I am sure God does not wish Gerardo to see what his son does. For if he did, he would die. Have you come to ransom them?

DIONISIO : I have sold all I can to cover it.

LIDORA : If only I could give them to you, Dionisio, but I cannot. It is true I became their mistress and they serve me but I myself am subject to the King. I am helpless.

GERARDO : It is not my wish to leave you, Lidora. I

would rather stay than leave you. In you,
Marcela has a sister, a true sister.

*Enter the* KING *and* ZULEMA, *dragging*
LEONIDO *by a rope.*

MARCELA: Now we are reunited. Take care, Dionisio. I
have never looked on this man without some
loss to myself or others.

ZARRAB.: See! A slave!

LEONIDO: I have a debt to pay. Father, sister. Oh, and
you, Dionisio. The runt has survived. And
Tizon awake at this hour? And Lidora picking
up Christian crumbs and comfort from the
servants' table?

KING: Lidora, I have done what you asked for. He's
brought in. I did it, only to please you. He's
about to die. Or, if you say so, not about to
die.

LIDORA: He is your prisoner. Just as I am yours.

LEONIDO: Father, I am at your feet, can you feel me? At
your feet. Can you hear me call you father?
You wished it once. Before I die, Father, note
this, note I am your son.

GERARDO: Son.

LEONIDO: By my mother, naturally. And naturally
raped, raped was the word I said, by you. As
I raped her in her turn. These are uneasy
times. Is that not what you would say, Father?
We live in troubled times, an age without
faith, the young go their sweet wild etcetera
ways. You cannot understand? Well, then: ah,
mother. She was pregnant. It was beyond
*your* doing. You were born old, like Dionisio
here. If Marcela drops another of us it will be
mine. My daughter. You see. I will explain.

59

It's simple enough before the bond's honoured.
We shall get there. Oh: first, she gave birth to
a little girl who was carried off in the jaws of
a she-bear. Ask me not how, but it is true. I
wanted to go after them but I didn't. My
mother was crying out. I left the she-bear and
went back to her and found there—
Marcela. New born and on the rock. Our
daughter. My sister.

MARCELA *collapses*.

Mark this. Marcela!

GERARDO : No—no more!

LEONIDO : It is quite enough. I am telling you so that
you may know what you have to ask pardon
for. For, oh yes, then I stabbed our wife, our
mother. You see. That, Father, is what
happened. Your tiny heart will not deny me
absolution?

KING : Zarrabulli! Take him where I told you.

LEONIDO : Lidora : I entrust all my family to you. You
will be busy. But you'll not mind. Remember
me a little longer.

ZARRABULLI *drags him out*.

MARCELA : Where has he gone?

KING : You will soon know, Lidora, I have given him
to you. Now, keep your word.

LIDORA : Very well, King. I am yours.

*The* KING *goes to take* LIDORA *in his arms*.

ZULEMA : Wait, Berlebeyo, before you do this, listen to
me. Before he died, your father the King gave
me this paper. I was to entrust it to no one
and I have not. You must read it before you
are betrothed.

KING : Read it.

60

ZULEMA *opens the charter.*

ZULEMA: It is in his father's own hand, Lidora. It reads, "Son, I hear of your wanting Lidora. I must tell you she is not your equal. When I was hunting Christians some sixteen years ago on the shores of Alicarte in Sicily, I rescued her from the mouth of a she-bear. She is a Christian and no match for my son. If you should marry her, our great Prophet Mahomet will rage against you. May Allah preserve you. Your father, Amete, Sultan".

KING: What? Oh, Divine Allah!

GERARDO: Divine heaven!

TIZON: If there's a Pope in Tunis he'll give him dispensation.

GERARDO: Quiet, fool! Lidora, you are really my daughter. This story tallies too well with Leonido's.

TIZON: Or well enough.

LIDORA: Oh, Gerardo. I have never known a father; it is better than the Kingdom of Tunis.

MARCELA: My dearest!

KING: Damn *all* fathers! Well, I am still King of Tunis. Tizon, bring Leonido here. If it is not too late. I think you should all be set free. And, well, persuaded to live together. It should be instructive.

*Enter* ZARRABULLI.

ZARRAB.: Oh, King, it is Argolan! See!

LEONIDO *hangs from a tree.*

LEONIDO: All of you . . . King, famous King. For you pay me like a King.

MARCELA: Leonido.

LEONIDO: Little sister.

61

GERARDO: My son.

LEONIDO: Bless you. Old toad!

GERARDO: Tizon, lead me to his body, My sight is
returning.

LEONIDO: Give him his sight. Tizon? Too drowsy?

TIZON *stabs him.*

Ah! If there is remembrance—I shall
remember you.

LIDORA: Berlebeyo, if you will let us, we will take this
body with us.

KING: Take it. Go. Bloody Christians, all of you.
Go. Back to Alicarte and your blood and
Sicily. Help them take him.

ZARRABULLI *and* TIZON *take up* LEONIDO.

TIZON: Well, King, he played a good tune on
vituperation. It may not be a bond honoured,
but it's a tune of sorts to end with.

*They drag him off.*

CURTAIN.